"The Kaleidoscope Mind: Embracing the Diversities in Poetic Collective"

By Deanna Starr

Introduction

Within the pages of "The Kaleidoscope Mind," an enchanting collection of poems awaits, offering a profound exploration of the diverse tapestry that is the human mind. Like the ever-shifting patterns of a kaleidoscope, these poems celebrate the myriad of thoughts, emotions, and perspectives that weave together to form our individuality.

"The Kaleidoscope Mind" invites you to embrace the kaleidoscope of thoughts, emotions, and experiences that make us uniquely human. Through the diverse range of poems found within this collection, dear readers, for you are encouraged to celebrate the beauty of our collective minds, each one a kaleidoscope of stories waiting to be shared.

Step into the enchanting realm of "The Kaleidoscope Mind," where the pages unfold like the ever-shifting patterns of a kaleidoscope, revealing the rich tapestry that constitutes the human mind. This collection of poems serves as a poetic voyage, inviting you to explore the diverse hues and intricacies that compose the landscape of our thoughts, emotions, and perspectives.

Much like the captivating dance of colors within a kaleidoscope, the poems in this collection are a celebration of the manifold aspects that define our individuality. From the vibrant to the subtle, the joyous to the contemplative, each verse is a brushstroke contributing to the masterpiece of the human mind.

As you delve into "The Kaleidoscope Mind," the invitation extended is not just to read but to actively participate in the celebration. It encourages you, dear readers, to revel in the beauty of our collective minds—a kaleidoscope of unique stories, each waiting to be uncovered and shared. These verses are not mere words; they are windows into the diverse narratives that shape our existence, beckoning you to join in the celebration of the human experience.

So, turn the pages with anticipation, for within this collection lies a journey that mirrors the complexities, joys, and wonders of the kaleidoscopic mind. Embrace the poetry that resonates with your own kaleidoscope, and let the shared stories within these verses become a symphony of voices, echoing the beauty of our collective human experience.

Within the pages of "The Kaleidoscope Mind," an enchanting collection of poems awaits, offering a profound exploration of the diverse tapestry that is the human mind. Like the ever-shifting patterns of a kaleidoscope, these poems celebrate the myriad of thoughts, emotions, and perspectives that weave together to form our individuality.

"The Kaleidoscope Mind" invites you to embrace the kaleidoscope of thoughts, emotions, and experiences that make us uniquely human. Through the diverse range of poems found within this collection, dear readers, for you are encouraged to celebrate the beauty of our collective minds, each one a kaleidoscope of stories waiting to be shared.

Step into the enchanting realm of "The Kaleidoscope Mind," where the pages unfold like the ever-shifting patterns of a kaleidoscope, revealing the rich tapestry that constitutes the human mind. This collection of poems serves as a poetic voyage, inviting you to explore the diverse hues and intricacies that compose the landscape of our thoughts, emotions, and perspectives.

Much like the captivating dance of colors within a kaleidoscope, the poems in this collection are a celebration of the manifold aspects that define our individuality. From the vibrant to the subtle, the joyous to the contemplative, each verse is a brushstroke contributing to the masterpiece of the human mind.

As you delve into "The Kaleidoscope Mind," the invitation extended is not just to read but to actively participate in the celebration. It encourages you, dear readers, to revel in the beauty of our collective minds—a kaleidoscope of unique stories, each waiting to be uncovered and shared. These verses are not mere words; they are windows into the diverse narratives that shape our existence, beckoning you to join in the celebration of the human experience.

So, turn the pages with anticipation, for within this collection lies a journey that mirrors the complexities, joys, and wonders of the kaleidoscopic mind. Embrace the poetry that resonates with your own kaleidoscope, and let the shared stories within these verses become a symphony of voices, echoing the beauty of our collective human experience.

CONTENTS

Introduction

Section One

"**The Kaleidoscope Mind: Embracing the Diversities in Poetic Collective**"

"**Metamorphosis of the Soul**"

"**Blossoming Souls: The Lotus Journey**"

"**Unveiling Brilliance: The Gemstone Journey**"

"**The Resilient Light: A Metaphorical Journey of Transformation**"

"**The Journey of Resilience: Illuminating Our Path**"

"**The Triumph of Self-Acceptance: Embracing Our Unique Light**"

"**The Tapestry of Mistakes: Stepping Stones to Greatness**"

"**God's Saving Grace: The Guiding Light in Life's Tapestry**"

"**Embracing Authenticity: Dancing to Our Own Beat**"

"**The Dance of Friendships: A Tapestry of Growth and Connection**"

"**Unveiling the Divine: A Journey of Self-Discovery**"

"**Divine Illumination: Unveiling the Light Within**"

"**Empath's Revelation: Embracing the Light Within**"

"**Lightworkers Starseeds Indigo Children: Awakening the Cosmic Consciousness**"

"**Harmony of the Divine: Embracing Love's Path**"

"**Voyage of the Poetic Nomad: Explorations in Metaphor and Existence**"

"**Invitation to Compassion: A Prelude to Caregiving Chronicles**"

"**Garden of Compassion: A Caregiver's Journey**"

Revised Poem: "**Harmony Unveiled: The Caregiver's Metamorphosis**"

"Love's Tapestry: An Enchanting Prelude"

"Symphony of Hearts: Love's Divine Brushstrokes"

"Dance of Life: A Tapestry of Work, Love, and Dreams"

"Harmony of Souls: A Symphony in Verse"

Section Two

"Cosmic Chronicles: A Meteor's Odyssey"

"Wings of Whimsy: A Butterfly's Tale"

"Wisdom's Horizon: A Philosophical Odyssey"

"Elysium of Imagination: A World Crafted in Dreams"

"Whispers of the Digital Realm: A Matrix Odyssey"

Section Three

"Thoughts in Technicolor"

"Whispers of the Soul"

"Reflections of the Unseen"

"Puzzle of Perspectives"

"Journeys of Imagination: Where Legends Unite"

"Inkblots of Identity"

"Whispers of the Kaleidoscope"

"Celestial Reverie: Wonders of the Universe"

"Prisms of Life: The Kaleidoscope of Human Experience."

"The Splendor of the Rainbow"

Section One

Step into a realm where words intertwine with emotions, where metaphors dance on the pages, and where the depths of the human experience are explored. Welcome to a book of poetic metaphors, a space filled with intrigue and thoughtfulness, designed to invite you, dear reader, to open your heart, mind, and the wonders within.

Within these pages, you will find a collection of verses that aim to touch the very core of your being. It is an invitation to delve into your own emotions, to unravel the threads of your thoughts and feelings, and to explore the hidden corners of your dreams. As you embark on this journey, you will be welcomed into my personal space, where my motivations, ideas, and theories come to life.

In the sanctuary of these metaphors, I share with you the whispers of my soul, the echoes of my experiences, and the reflections of my imagination. It is a place where vulnerability meets strength, where pain intertwines with hope, and where the power of words has the ability to ignite the spark of understanding within.

So, dear reader, I invite you to surrender to the enchantment of these poetic metaphors. Open your heart wide and let the words seep in, for within them, you may discover a mirror to your own journey, a catalyst for introspection, and a companion on the path of self-discovery.

May these words ignite the fire within you, stir the depths of your emotions, and inspire you to embrace the infinite possibilities that lie within your own personal space. Let us embark on this poetic adventure together, where the power of metaphors allows us to connect, to reflect, and to dream.

Let us begin by exploring a metaphor of a person being compared to the transformative journey of a butterfly.

"Metamorphosis of the Soul"

Just like a butterfly, a person's life unfolds,
Through stages of growth, their story is told.
From humble beginnings, they start their quest,
Transforming and evolving, they give it their best.

Like a caterpillar, they explore and learn,
Feeding on knowledge, their desire to discern.
They stretch their limits, reaching for the sky,
Building a strong foundation as time goes by.

Then, in their chrysalis, they find a space,
A time for reflection, a moment to embrace.
They shed their old self, leaving behind the past,
Preparing for the future, they must adapt and cast.

And finally, they emerge, transformed and new,
A person of beauty, with a different view.
Their experiences, like colors on their wings,
Tell a story of growth, of all the joy it brings.

They soar through life, with confidence and grace,
Inspiring others in their own unique space.
Their journey, a metaphor for us all to see,
That transformation is possible for you and me.

So, embrace your transformations, like a butterfly's flight,
Let your true colors shine, with all your might.
For just like this creature, your journey will unfold,
And you'll find the beauty in being transformed and bold.

In the tapestry of life, 'Blossoming Souls: The Lotus Journey' unfolds as a metaphorical exploration of human resilience and self-discovery. Much like the lotus rising from murky waters, this poem delves into the transformative journey of individuals facing challenges, blooming with strength, and radiating inner beauty.

Let the verses guide you through a poetic reflection on growth, balance, and the profound worth of every moment.

"Blossoming Souls: The Lotus Journey"

Imagine a person, like a lotus in a pond,
Their transformative journey, profound and beyond.
From the depths, they rise, with roots firmly planted,
Growing towards the Light, where dreams are enchanted.

Just like the lotus, they face challenges and strife,
But they find strength within, to navigate life.
Through muddy waters, they rise above the mire,
Blooming with resilience, their spirits inspire.

At first, a seed buried deep in the Earth,
They face adversity, seeking self-worth.
But as they grow, their potential unfurls,
Petals opening, revealing their inner pearls.

They embrace the journey of self-discovery,
Unfolding layers of their own mystery.
With each passing day, they blossom and bloom,
Radiating beauty, dispelling any gloom.

Like the lotus, they find serenity and peace,
Amidst chaos and turmoil, their worries release.
They teach us to find balance and harmony,
Embracing growth, just like the lotus does gracefully.

Their transformation, a symbol of rebirth,
A reminder to embrace life's infinite worth.
Through every challenge, they rise above,
Transforming into a reflection of self-love.

So, let us learn from the lotus, serene and strong,
To face life's trials and sing our own song.
Embrace the transformative journey we're on,
And like the lotus, let our spirits dawn.

Let's delve into the metaphor of a person being compared to the transformative journey of a precious gemstone:

"Unveiling Brilliance: The Gemstone Journey"

Imagine a person, like a precious gemstone rare,
With layers of potential waiting to be brought to bear.
Like a diamond, they start as a rough, unpolished stone,
But through life's pressures, they find their true tone.

Just like a gem, they face the cutting and grinding,
To reveal their brilliance, their true worth shining.
Each facet represents a lesson learned,
As they navigate life's twists and turns.

At first, they may appear ordinary and plain,
But with time and effort, they can truly gain.
They endure the heat and pressure of life's trials,
Transforming into something that truly beguiles.

As they embrace their journey, they find inner strength,
Polishing their character, going to any length.
Each challenge they conquer, each setback they face,
Adds to their beauty, their essence, their grace.

Through the process of growth, they become refined,
Reflecting the Light, their true brilliance defined.
Their flaws and imperfections, seen as unique,
Enhancing their worth, making them truly chic.

Just like a gemstone, they hold great value within,
A testament to their resilience and the battles they win.
They teach us to embrace our own transformation,
To shine bright, despite any limitations.

So, let us learn from the gemstone's transformative power,
To embrace life's challenges, and never cower.
Just like a gem, let us uncover our true potential,
And radiate brilliance, becoming truly exceptional.

The introduction to the journey…

"The Resilient Light: A Metaphorical Journey of Transformation"

Imagine a metaphorical journey that encapsulates the profound intensities of life's experiences. Picture a young child, innocent and tender, growing into an adult, then reaching the middle-aged phase of existence. Along this path, the person is picked out, bullied, and subjected to unfair and unkind treatment. It is a transformative journey marked by hardships and struggles that seem never-ending.

Yet, in the depths of this metaphorical voyage lies a revelation. Through the trials and tribulations, the individual perseveres, refusing to give up or surrender. Each challenge faced becomes a refining process, molding them into a resilient being. And amidst the darkness, a realization emerges – all the struggle and adversity have served to refine their essence, to shape them into a brightly shining light.

This Light, borne out of resilience and unwavering determination, stands tall with pride, undeterred by the storms that once threatened to break them. It becomes a beacon of inspiration, a testament to the strength found within. Through the metaphorical journey of this individual, we are reminded that even in the face of adversity, we have the capacity to rise above, to embrace our inner Light, and to become an embodiment of triumph.

So, let us passionately, deeply, and emotionally grasp the intensities of this metaphorical exploration. Let us celebrate the transformative power of resilience and the beauty that emerges from the struggles we face. May this journey inspire us to never lose hope, to keep pushing forward, and to ultimately become the shining lights that illuminate our own paths and inspire others along the way.

"The Journey of Resilience: Illuminating Our Path"

In the realm of metaphorical dreams,
A journey unfolds, or so it seems.
From a young child's innocent gaze,
To an adult's wisdom, earned through days.

A life, once adorned with tender grace,
Transforms as time reveals its face.
Bullied and treated unfairly, unkind,
A struggle emerges battles to find.

Through darkness and hardships, they persist,
Never surrendering, persistently resist.
Each trial, a refining fire's embrace,
Shaping character with every trace.

And as the storms rage, they endure,
Their spirit is unyielding, strong and pure.
A brightly shining light emerges: bright,
A symbol of triumph, a radiant sight.

Standing tall, with pride, they beam,
A beacon of strength, a hopeful gleam.
For all the struggles, the pain, the strife,
Have sculpted a soul, a resilient life.

Oh, the beauty that emerges from within,
When life's adversities are faced and pinned.
From young child to an adult's embrace,
They've become the embodiment of grace.

So let us grasp this imagery profound,
Of a transformative journey, so renowned.
May it inspire us to never give in,
To rise above and let our own Light begin.

For within each of us resides the power,
To endure, to thrive, to blossom and flower.
From young to old, through every stage,
We can be the shining lights on life's grand stage.

"The Triumph of Self-Acceptance: Embracing Our Unique Light"

In the depths of longing and sorrow,
Where pain and comparison borrow,
A metaphoric tale takes flight,
Of sisters, divided by favor's might.

The oldest, burdened by the weight,
Of never being the chosen, the one to elate,
She yearns for recognition, a chance to be seen,
In a world where her worth feels unseen.

But amidst the shadows, a spark emerges,
A flicker of resilience, as her spirit surges,
She learns to embrace her own unique Light,
To rise above the pain with all her might.

This poem delves into the depths of her soul,
Where the pain of never being whole,
Is transformed into strength and grace,
A journey of self-discovery, in this sacred space.

In a realm of shadows, where pain resides,
Lies a tale of sisters, where comparison divides.
The oldest, a flower, once vibrant and bold,
Now wilted and fragile, her heart left cold.

Through life's prism, she watches with despair,
As favor graces others, leaving her in the air.
Her worth diminished, like whispers in the wind,
The pain of never being the one deeply chagrined.

She yearns for recognition, a moment to shine,
To feel the warmth of love, like sweet sunshine.
But destiny's hand seems cruel and unkind,
Leaving her to bear the burden, left behind.

And then, a third sister enters the scene,

With favor bestowed upon her, like a queen.
The oldest sister's pain, now multiplied,
As she witnesses another's success, side by side.

Oh, how it cuts deep, the sting of comparison,
A constant reminder of her never-ending omission.
She questions her worth, her very existence,
Longing for a chance to break free from resistance.

But in the depth of her sorrow, a spark ignites,
A flicker of resilience, refusing to dim her lights.
For she is more than the favor she receives,
Her spirit, unyielding, refuses to believe.

With each passing day, she finds strength anew,
Embracing her essence, her soul's brilliant hue.
No longer defined by others' fleeting acclaim,
She rises from the ashes, igniting her own flame.

For in the symphony of life, her part shall play,
A melody of resilience in her own unique way.
She learns to cherish her journey, despite the pain,
To find solace in the wisdom she shall gain.

So, dear oldest sister, let not your spirit wane,
Let not comparison's shadow forever stain.
You are a masterpiece in your own divine right,
Unfolding your story with courage and might.

Embrace the beauty that lies deep within,
For your worth goes beyond the favor you win.
In your own time, you shall shine bright,
A beacon of strength through the darkest night.

In the tapestry of life, mistakes often weave themselves into our stories, leaving us with scars and lessons learned. But what if these mistakes, instead of defining us, could become stepping stones towards a brighter future? This metaphoric poem explores the transformative power of mistakes, as they shape and prepare us for greater times ahead.

"The Tapestry of Mistakes: Stepping Stones to Greatness"

In the realm of mistakes, a tapestry unfolds,
Where lessons lie hidden, waiting to be told.
Each misstep, a thread in life's grand design,
Leading us closer to greatness, divine.

The first misstep, a stumble in the dark,
A lesson learned: a fire to spark,
For in failure's embrace, we find the key,
To unlock the potential within you and me.

As we journey on, mistakes in our wake,
The path becomes clearer, our resolve awake.
With each wrong turn, a map to be drawn,
Guiding us towards the dawn of a new dawn.

For the mistakes we make, though painful and tough,
Carry the seeds of resilience, more than enough.
They mold us, shape us, and make us whole,
Preparing us for greatness with heart and soul.

So, embrace the missteps, the errors, and falls,
For they are the stepping stones to higher walls.
With every mistake, a lesson to glean,
In preparation for the greatness, we've yet to dream.

In this tapestry of life, mistakes are not in vain,
But rather the fuel that ignites the flame,
To rise above, to soar, to reach the skies,
With lessons learned, our spirits forever rise.

Life is a journey full of twists and turns, joys and sorrows. But what if we had a guiding force, a beacon of Light that never wavered? This metaphorical poem explores the profound impact of God's saving grace in our lives. It celebrates the blessed assurance of His presence, His guiding hands, and His comforting voice, which accompany us every step of the way. Let us embrace the gratitude for the unwavering presence of God in our lives.

"God's Saving Grace: The Guiding Light in Life's Tapestry"

In the tapestry of life, God's grace unfolds,
A beacon of hope, a love that never molds.
With each step I take, His guiding hands I feel,
His voice whispers softly, assuring me it's real.

Without His saving grace, life's path is obscure,
A tumultuous journey, uncertain and impure.
But with Him by my side, I walk with confidence and peace,
For His love never falters. It only continues to increase.

Through valleys of darkness, His Light shines bright,
He leads me gently, with His love as my guiding Light.
In moments of doubt, His voice speaks clear,
Reassuring me that He is always near.

With gratitude in my heart, I give thanks each day,
For His unwavering presence, never astray.
In times of joy and times of strife,
I find solace in God's saving grace, the essence of life.

So let us cherish His love, His mercy, and His care,
For God is always with us, our burdens He will bear.
In His presence, we find peace, strength, and embrace,
The blessed assurance of His saving grace.

With every breath I take, I'm thankful and aware,
That God is with me, always loving and always there.
In this journey of life, His grace is my constant guide,
With Him by my side, I'll forever abide.

In a world where conformity often reigns, where societal expectations and pressures can stifle our true selves, there is a yearning within us all to break free. We embark on a journey of self-discovery, seeking to find our own unique identity, to embrace our individuality, and to celebrate the power of being true to ourselves. In this poem, I invite you to join me on this journey as we delve into the depths of self-reflection and let our inner Light shine. Let us dance to the beat of our own drum and, together, create a world where authenticity and uniqueness are celebrated.

"Embracing Authenticity: Dancing to Our Own Beat"

In the vast expanse of time's embrace,
From birth to fifty, I've embarked on a chase,
A journey of self-discovery, of finding my way,
Amidst the influence of others who had their say.

But who am I, in contrast to their desires?
A unique soul fueled by passions, raging fires,
I am not a follower nor a leader in the crowd,
I dance to my own beat, standing tall and proud.

Like the stars that adorn the galaxies above,
I shine bright, independent, a symbol of love,
Not lonely or sad, but joyful and content,
For I've embraced my uniqueness, my spirit unbent.

No victim am I, nor do I demand entitlements,
For I've created my own worth, my own strengths,
I am strong and creative, with a mind of my own,
Guided by the Light of the galaxies, I have grown.

The galaxies, pure and vast, hold secrets untold,
They show me their guidance, both night and bold,
In their twinkling lights, I find solace and peace,
A reminder that my journey's purpose will never cease.

So let me continue on this path, unswayed,
Embracing my individuality, never afraid,
For in the depths of self-discovery, I strive,
To shine brightly, like the stars, and truly thrive.

And as I navigate the years that lie ahead,
I'll remain true to myself, no compromises, no dread,
For I am the author of my own destiny,
A soul that dances to its own unique melody.

In the realm of friendships, a tapestry of experiences unfolds, weaving together the values we hold dear and the hidden lessons we encounter along the way. It is within the bonds of friendship that we witness the ebb and flow of change, as some relationships blossom and flourish while others gently drift apart. This journey of friendship is a mirror that reflects not only who we were but who we are and who we aspire to become.

And now, allow me to present to you a heartfelt poem that delves into the intricate tapestry of friendships, exploring the essence of growth, connection, and self-discovery.

"The Dance of Friendships: A Tapestry of Growth and Connection"

In the dance of friendships, a tale unfolds,
Of values shared and stories yet untold.
Weaving together a tapestry of years,
Embracing the laughter, the joy, the tears.

Through seasons of change, we find our way,
Growing together, come what may.
Like branches swaying in the gentle breeze,
Friendships evolve like whispers in the trees.

Some friendships blossom, radiant and bright,
Guiding us towards our inner Light.
With kindred spirits, we find solace and grace,
A bond that time and distance can't erase.

But as the tides of life ebb and flow,
Some friendships drift like seeds we sow.
Paths diverge, leading us astray,
Yet memories linger forever in our hearts they stay.

For in the realm of friendships, we find,
Lessons hidden in the ties that bind.
Through joys and sorrows, we come to see,
The beauty of growth and who we're meant to be.

So, cherish each connection, dear and true,
For friendships shape and mold us through and through.
Discover who you were, who you are, who you'll be,
For friendships hold the key to setting your spirit free.

"Unveiling the Divine: A Journey of Self-Discovery"

In the vast tapestry of existence, there is a profound need to know who we truly are - divine and unique creations of God. This poem is a passionate exploration of that yearning, urging us to delve deep within ourselves and uncover the essence that sets us apart. It invites us to embrace our true identity, to acknowledge our strengths and weaknesses, and to embark on a journey of self-discovery. Through vivid imagery and heartfelt words, this poem celebrates the beauty of our individuality and reminds us that we are all masterpieces, intricately woven by the hands of the Divine.

In a world filled with noise and distraction,
There lies a yearning, a deep satisfaction.
A need to uncover the essence within,
To know your purpose, to let your Light begin.

For you, my dear, are a divine creation,
Fashioned by God, with love and dedication.
A masterpiece crafted with delicate care,
With gifts and talents beyond compare.

In the depths of your soul, there's a fire ablaze,
A spark of uniqueness that sets you ablaze.
No one else in this world is quite like you,
A tapestry of colors, vibrant and true.

Seek not the validation of others' eyes,
But delve within, where your true self lies.
Embrace the quirks, the flaws, and the grace,
For they form the fabric of your unique space.

Discover the passions that ignite your soul,
Let them guide you on a journey untold.
For in the pursuit of self-discovery,
You'll unlock the door to your true identity.

Embrace the shadows, the doubts, and the fears,
For they too hold lessons, and wipe away tears.
You are a force, both gentle and wild,
An embodiment of dreams, God's precious child.

So, dare to explore the depths of your being,
Unravel the layers, for there's no ceiling.
Embrace the adventure as life unfolds,
And let your true self, ever more, be bold.

For in knowing who you are, my dear,
You'll find the freedom, the purpose, so clear.
Embrace the journey, embrace the call,
For you are divine, the most beautiful of all.

"Divine Illumination: Unveiling the Light Within"

In the realm of poetry, where words intertwine,
A short introduction: let me now align.
This poem explores the essence of God's Light,
Guiding our souls, forever burning bright.

With passion and depth, let us embark,
On a journey of words, where meaning sparks.
Within these verses, we shall uncover,
The beauty and grace of the divine cover.

So, join me now as we dive right in,
To a world of wonder, where faith begins.
This poem unveils the power and might,
Of God's eternal Light, shining so bright.

In the depths of darkness, where shadows reside,
We find a flicker of hope, a radiant guide.
For God is the Light, a celestial flame,
Burning within us, igniting our name.

In the vastness of space, where galaxies swirl,
We are but stardust, a celestial pearl.
With the essence of divinity, we are blessed,
To carry His Light on this earthly quest.

Through trials and tribulations, when all seems lost,

We summon His strength, no matter the cost.
For within us resides a spark divine,
A beacon of love that eternally shines.

In the darkest corners, where despair holds sway,
We shall not falter; we shall not dismay.
For we are bearers of His divine grace,
Illuminating paths with every embrace.

Like stars in the night, we shall brightly gleam,
Dispelling the darkness with a radiant beam.
In words and actions, we share His pure Light,
Guiding lost souls towards love's resolute might.

With compassion as our compass, we shall lead,
Unveiling His glory, fulfilling our creed.
In unity, we stand as His chosen kin,
Radiating His love, breaking through every sin.

Let us be the lighthouse, standing tall and strong,
Guiding lost ships when the night is long.
For He is the Light, the source of our might,
And through us, His radiance shines ever bright.

So let our hearts be the torches that ignite,
The fire of love dispelling the night.
Let us be the Light, both near and far,
For within us, God's divine presence does spar.

In unity, we rise like a blazing sun,
With love as our armor, we've already won.
For in His image, we are created true,
Beacons of hope, shining brightly through.

So let us embrace our purpose, our call,
To shine His Light, illuminating all.
For God is the Light, forever and always,
And within us, His love eternally plays.

"Empath's Revelation: Embracing the Light Within"

In the depths of chaos, where bad choices thrived,
A revelation emerged, and my soul revived.
An empath's awakening, a light so profound,
This metaphorical journey, let it astound.

In the realm of tangled thoughts, chaos reigned,
My life, a labyrinth of bad choices, stained.
Yet amidst the mess, a flicker of Light,
An empath's awakening, shining so bright.

Like a hidden gem, unknown and unseen,
The revelation came a mystical dream.
A key to unlock the mysteries within,
To understand myself, where to begin.

As an empath, I walk a different path,
Sensing emotions, feeling others' wrath.
But with this newfound knowledge, I found peace,
A beacon guiding me, granting release.

Imagine a garden, overgrown and wild,
Each thorny thicket, my thoughts beguiled.
Yet, as I embraced my empathic grace,
The garden transformed a sacred space.

With every step, weeds cleared from my way,
The messes and troubles began to sway.
Empathy, a healer, a transformative force,
Liberating my soul, setting a new course.

Like a phoenix rising, I soared above,
Embracing my gifts, expanding with love.
Stronger each day, like a mighty oak,
Rooted in empathy, a foundation spoke.

Now, I navigate the world, empathic and wise,
With an open heart and understanding eyes.
My mind, once cluttered, now serene and clear,

The Light of empathy banishing all fear.

So let us celebrate this metaphoric tale,
Of an empath's journey, a triumphant sail.
May we all find solace in knowing who we are,
Embracing our essence, shining like a star.

Short explainable.
Lightworkers is a term used to describe individuals who are spiritually awakened and dedicated to spreading love, healing, and positivity in the world. They are often seen as individuals who work with the metaphysical and spiritual realms to bring about positive change.

While lightworkers can be individuals of any religious or spiritual background, including Christianity, the term itself is not specific to any particular religious belief. Lightworkers may draw inspiration from various spiritual traditions and philosophies, incorporating teachings from different sources into their practice.

The concept of lightworkers aligns with the idea of being instruments of God's love and guidance in the world. They strive to bring about positive transformation, uplift others, and promote healing, all while embodying qualities such as compassion, kindness, and empathy. Lightworkers believe in the power of love, the interconnectedness of all beings, and the importance of spiritual growth.

In Christianity, the concept of being a lightworker can be related to the teachings of Jesus Christ, who encouraged his followers to be the Light of the world and spread God's love to others. Christians who identify as lightworkers may see their work as an expression of their faith and a way to fulfill their calling to serve God and humanity.

Ultimately, whether someone identifies as a lightworker or not, what truly matters is the intention behind their actions and the values they uphold. It is important to remember that different individuals may interpret and express their spirituality in various ways. The most important aspect is the alignment with love, compassion, and the pursuit of goodness, regardless of the specific term used.

"Lightworkers Starseeds Indigo Children: Awakening the Cosmic Consciousness"

In the realm of ethereal whispers, where souls intertwine,
Reside the Light Workers, vessels of divine design.
They are the cosmic alchemists, weaving threads of Light,
Transmuting shadows into gold, with powers infinite.

Starseeds, celestial travelers from realms unknown,
Sent on interstellar winds, their purpose finely honed.
They carry stardust in their veins, a celestial birthright,
Navigating earthly realms, guided by cosmic starlight.

Indigo Children, with auras ablaze, like a prism's hue,
Born with ancient wisdom, in their eyes, it shines through.
They possess the keys to unlock universal truths,
Awakening consciousness, igniting spiritual pursuits.

Light Workers, Starseeds, Indigo Children intertwined,
Silent warriors of spirit, their presence softly defined.
They are the healers, mending souls with tender care,
Healing scars unseen, igniting flames of love's affair.

With hearts aglow, they radiate compassion's embrace,
Transcending boundaries, connecting every race.
Their souls dance with the moon, their spirits soaring high,
Guiding humanity's journey to ascend the sky.

Embrace your inner Light Worker, Starseed, Indigo Child,
Embody the cosmic symphony, let it run wild.
For you are a vessel of Divine Light, a sacred flame,
Transforming darkness into brilliance in love's holy name.

So let your spirit soar like a phoenix taking flight,
Shedding layers of doubt, embracing your inner Light.
In this celestial tapestry, we all play our part,
To awaken the world's consciousness with love as our art.

"Harmony of the Divine: Embracing Love's Path"

Ah, the Alpha and Omega, the eternal essence,
A guiding force beyond human comprehension.
In the realm of spirituality, where paths converge,
The Divine presence, like a sacred surge.

The question of alignment with the Divine,
A query that resonates, seeking a sign.
For each soul's journey, unique and vast,
The answer lies within, a truth to grasp.

God, the Alpha and Omega, the source of all,
Transcends labels beyond earthly walls.
In the tapestry of existence, we all play a role,
Connected and intertwined, one divine whole.

To align with God, the cosmic symphony,
Is to embody love, in its purest form, you see.
To radiate compassion, kindness, and grace,
Embracing unity in every corner of space.

It is to honor the sacredness of all life,
To nurture the soul amidst turmoil and strife.
To seek truth and wisdom with an open heart,
And let love guide your actions right from the start.

The path to alignment is not a single road,
But a journey of growth, a story yet untold.
It's about finding your purpose, your unique role,
And living in harmony with your divine soul.

So, dear seeker, as you navigate this quest,
Remember, God's love is boundless, the very best.
Align with the essence of love, let it flow,
And you shall find your path, the way to grow.

For in the realm of the Alpha and Omega,
We are all connected in love's grand opera.
So, walk your path with faith, let love be your guide,
And in alignment with God, may your spirit truly reside.

Step into the realm of inspiration and imagination, where words dance with metaphors and emotions and paint vibrant landscapes. Prepare to embark on a poetic journey guided by a traveler who has experienced life's tapestry firsthand. In this introduction, allow your mind to wander and your heart to open as the beauty of metaphorical poetry unfolds before you. Get ready to explore the depths of existence, traverse cosmic landscapes, and delve into the realms of emotions and spirituality. Let the symphony of words ignite your imagination and awaken your sense of wonder. Open your mind, for this is a poetic voyage that will leave you inspired and longing for more.

As a traveler on the path of existence, let us paint a metaphorical portrait of this experience:

"Voyage of the Poetic Nomad: Explorations in Metaphor and Existence"

I am but a wanderer lost amidst the cosmic expanse,
A solitary star embarking on a dance.
Time, a whispering wind, caresses my weary soul,
Unveiling the stories that the universe holds.

I traverse the galaxies, a nomad of mystic flight,
Each realm is a kaleidoscope, a celestial delight.
Through the tapestry of space, I find my way,
Exploring the dimensions where realities sway.

Emotions, like a tempest, surge within my core,
A symphony of colors, a sea of emotions, I soar.
Love, a gentle breeze, wraps me in its warm embrace,
While sadness, a torrential rain, washes away my grace.

In the depths of consciousness, I delve with curiosity,
A realm of endless wonder, an ethereal sanctuary.
Thoughts intertwined like vines, weaving dreams and schemes,
A tapestry of ideas where inspiration gleams.

Spirituality, a compass guiding my quest,
A flame that burns within, a divinely blessed crest.

Beliefs and faith ignite the flame, a sacred fire,
Guiding me through the dimensions, higher and higher.
In this metaphorical journey, I am the poet, the muse,
Weaving words like threads, painting scenes anew.
Experiencing existence in its manifold form,
Immersed in the cosmic symphony, forever reborn.

Oh, to be the protagonist, the witness, the seer,
To embrace the multidimensional truth, crystal clear.
For in this firsthand experience, I find liberation,
And immerse myself in life's poetic revelation.

"Invitation to Compassion: A Prelude to Caregiving Chronicles"

In the realm of care and compassion, where hearts beat in unison, and hands reach out to uplift others, lies a place of extraordinary significance. It is a realm where the power of healing and support intertwines with the boundless potential of human connection. It is within this realm that I extend an invitation to you to embark on a transformative journey of caregiving.

In this realm, you will discover the profound impact that your presence can have on the lives of those in need. Whether it be through lending a listening ear, offering a helping hand, or providing comfort in times of distress, your contributions will become the pillars of strength that others rely upon.

Yet, this journey is not one embarked upon solely for the benefit of others. It is a path that holds immense personal growth and fulfillment. As you immerse yourself in the act of caring for others, you will witness the remarkable resilience of the human spirit. You will come to understand the depths of empathy and kindness that reside within you, and you will witness the transformative power of love and compassion.

In this realm, the impact of your actions will extend far beyond the boundaries of time and space. The ripple effect of your care will touch lives that you may never meet, and your legacy will continue to inspire and uplift future generations. Every act of kindness, no matter how small, has the potential to ignite a spark of hope and ignite a flame of change.

So, my dear friend, I extend this invitation to you with utmost sincerity. Step into this realm of caregiving, where your presence will make a difference, your actions will redefine lives, and your heart will find solace in the knowledge that you are making the world a better place. Embrace this journey of compassion, for in doing so, you will not only transform the lives of others but also discover the profound beauty of your own existence.

"Garden of Compassion: A Caregiver's Journey"

In the vast garden of life, a caregiver emerges,
Nurturing the frail blossoms, the aging souls,
With hands gentle and hearts overflowing,
They embark on a journey, a gift untold.

Day one dawns, like a fragile seedling,
Unsure of the path but carrying hope's glow,
The caregiver tends to each tender need,
Watering with compassion, watching them grow.

Like a sprout reaching for the sun's embrace,
They learn to navigate the intricacies of care,
Through long nights and weary days,
Their dedication blooms, unwavering and rare.

Each interaction, a delicate dance of trust,
As they cradle memories like petals in their hands,
They listen, they comfort, they hold space,
Guiding their charges through life's shifting sands.

Through the seasons of life, they witness it all,
The laughter, the tears, the stories untold,
From childhood memories to the wisdom of old,
Each moment cherished a tapestry to behold.

And as the caregiver matures, like an ancient tree,
Rooted in wisdom, branches reaching the sky,
They become the shelter, the shade, the strength,
A beacon of love as time continues to fly.

Retirement beckons, a bittersweet farewell,
Leaving behind a legacy, a garden of care,
For the seeds they planted have blossomed,
Their impact is forever woven beyond compare.

In the growth of the caregiver, a transformation unfolds,
From a tender bud to a resilient bloom,

They have nurtured, they have grown,
Leaving behind a trail of love in every room.

For the caregiver's journey is one of grace,
Their compassion is a beacon in a world often cold,
May their story inspire, ignite the hearts,
To honor and cherish the elderly as the ages unfold.

Revised Poem: "Harmony Unveiled: The Caregiver's Metamorphosis"

In the tapestry of life, there exists a role,
A caregiver's journey, both humble and bold,
With hands that hold and hearts that heal,
They embark on a path where compassion is revealed.

Imagine a garden where time softly weaves,
A caregiver's story, where love never leaves,
From day one to retirement, a metamorphosis unfolds,
As they tend to the elderly, their wisdom takes hold.

Like a seedling in the soil, their journey begins,
With uncertain steps but a fire within,
They enter the realm of caregiving's embrace,
To nurture the aging souls, with tenderness and grace.

From the first encounter, a bond starts to bloom,
As they listen to stories in the quiet of the room,
With hands that comfort and voices that soothe,
They become the pillars for those seeking truth.

Through long nights and weary days, they persist,
With unwavering dedication, their spirits insist,
To be a guiding light, in the twilight years,
As they wipe away sorrows and conquer fears.

Like a sprout reaching for the sun's golden rays,
They navigate the challenges, in myriad ways,
Each interaction, a dance of empathy and care,
As they walk hand in hand, with those needing repair.

Seasons change as time paints its hues,
And the caregiver's heart, forever renews,
From childhood memories to life's lessons learned,
They hold the wisdom that the aging have earned.

And as they retire, like a grand tree standing tall,
Their legacy remains, like a gentle recall,
For the seeds they planted, have blossomed and grown,
Their impact lingers in the hearts they have known.

This is the tale of a caregiver's rise,
A journey of compassion, where love never dies,
May their story inspire, ignite the hearts anew,
To honor the elderly, and the caregivers too.

"Love's Tapestry: An Enchanting Prelude"

In the tapestry of love's enchanting realm, there exists a myriad of actions that weave together the beautiful fabric of a relationship. Through this inspiring metaphoric poem, we embark on a journey where love manifests itself in countless ways, illuminating the path of our hearts. From the profound bond between spouses to the cherished friendship between kindred souls, we explore the power of helping hands, shared tasks, listening ears, gentle touches, and the joyous unity in activities and entertainment.

In this poetic exploration, we discover that love is not confined to grand gestures alone, but rather, it flourishes in the intricate tapestry of everyday moments. With each line, we are reminded of the profound impact we can have on our loved ones through the simplest of actions. This poem serves as a reminder to cherish the beauty in the mundane, to infuse love into every aspect of our lives, and to create a love that stands proud and tall, like a masterpiece of the heart.

"Symphony of Hearts: Love's Divine Brushstrokes"

In the realm of love, where hearts entwine,
A symphony of actions, so divine.
For our spouse, our friend, our dearest love,
We embark on a journey, guided from above.

With helping hands, we ease life's strain,
Shouldering burdens, relieving pain.
Shared tasks become a dance of grace,

Together we conquer any challenge we face.
Listening ears, attuned to every word,
Understanding the thoughts, however absurd.
In silence, we find solace and peace,
A sanctuary where worries cease.

Like a gentle touch, a soft caress,
We nurture and comfort; we heal and bless.
In every embrace, a language untold,
Love's warmth and tenderness treasure to behold.

As we join in activities, both big and small,
Creating memories, forging bonds that never fall.
Around the house, a haven we create,
Where love blossoms and dreams resonate.

Entertainments become moments of delight,
Laughter dancing in the starry night.
In shared laughter, joy finds its wings,
And in unity, our love sings.

So let us be inspired, let us be bold,
In the actions we take, love to unfold.
For in these gestures, both big and small,
We build a love that stands proud and tall.

In the realm of love, where hearts ignite,
We paint a masterpiece, a love so bright.
With each action, a brushstroke divine,
Creating a love that will forever shine.

In the realm of life's intricate tapestry, there exists a poem that beautifully encapsulates the quest for balance. It is a heartfelt expression of one's journey in seeking harmony amidst the demands of work, the commitments of marriage, and the pursuit of personal dreams. This poem serves as a reminder of the delicate dance we ALL partake in, as we strive to find equilibrium in the hustle and bustle of everyday life. Through its words, it paints a vivid picture of the challenges faced and the resilience displayed while offering a glimmer of hope and inspiration. Join me as we delve into the depths of this poetic exploration, where the protagonist's determination and unwavering spirit shine through, illuminating the path towards a life well-lived.

"Dance of Life: A Tapestry of Work, Love, and Dreams"

In the realm of time's intricate dance,
A life unfolds, a delicate balance to enhance.
Between work's demands and dreams that ignite,
A marriage thrives love's eternal Light.

With every passing day, the clock ticks away,
Yet I navigate this maze with grace.
In the realm of responsibilities, I hold my ground,
Juggling commitments so astoundingly profound.

From the early morn till the night's embrace,
I conquer the challenges that life does chase.
Diligently tending to work's demanding call,
I give my all, never fearing to fall.

But amidst the chaos, I never forget,
That dreams are the fuel that keeps my soul set.
In those stolen moments, when time slows its pace,
I chase after my dreams, leaving no trace.

And in the sacred bond of marriage's sweet embrace,
I find solace and love, a harmonious space.
Together, we navigate life's winding path,
Supporting each other, warding off any wrath.

So, my dear, let me remind myself now,
That my journey is remarkable, this I vow.
The symphony I conduct, with love and care,
Creates a life worth cherishing beyond compare.

In the grand tapestry of life's intricate design,
I weave my dreams, my work, our love entwined.
With a heart full of courage and a spirit so bright,
I conquer the odds, shining with radiant Light.

So, I will embrace this dance of time with all my might,
For I, my dear, am a beacon of strength and Light.
May my journey be filled with joy and bliss,

As I balance work, marriage, and the dreams I can't resist.

I write this as an encouragement and recognition that will be an affirmation as well as a manifestation for continuous strength and blessing. So, when you read it, make it yours.

"Harmony of Souls: A Symphony in Verse"

Open your hearts and minds, dear reader, to a world
Where music weaves its enchantment, unfurled.
Let these words resonate, echo within your soul,
As we embark on a journey, where emotions unfold.

Immerse yourself in the symphony of these lines,
Where each verse beckons, a call that intertwines.
Pause for a moment, let the rhythm take hold,
And let the melodies within you be uncontrolled.

For this is not just a poem, a mere collection of words,
But an invitation to feel, to be stirred.
Let the resonance of these verses ignite a flame,
As we explore the power of music, its an eternal aim.

With each stanza, let your spirit soar,
And through the verses, let your heart explore.
May these words connect, resonate deep within,
As we celebrate the magic that music can begin.

So, dear reader, with an open heart, I implore,
Immerse yourself in this musical lore.
Let the symphony of these words guide your way,
And may the harmony of life's song forever stay.

In the depths of our existence, where mind and soul entwine,
Lies a symphony of emotions, a celestial design.
For within the chambers of our being, a melody does flow,
Music, the ethereal language, where healing energies bestow.

Imagine, if you will, our minds as vast orchestras,
Each thought, an instrument, playing harmonious cadenzas.

"The Kaleidoscope Mind: Embracing the Diversities in Poetic Collective"   By Deanna F Starr

The strings of reason, plucked with delicate precision,
The brass of passion, resounding with fiery intuition.

And in this grand symphony, our souls become the maestro,
Conducting the rhythm of life, where emotions freely flow.
With each note that resonates, a spectrum of colors arise,
Painting the canvas of our existence, a masterpiece in disguise.

For music, dear friend, holds the power to heal the wounds we bear,
Its tender embrace, a balm that mends with utmost care.
With every gentle chord, it whispers to our weary souls,
Guiding us through the darkness, making us feel whole.

In times of sorrow, it weaves a lullaby so sweet,
Wrapping us in its embrace, a refuge from defeat.
Each melancholic note, a tearful release,
Cleansing the burdens, granting us inner peace.

Yet music is not limited to sorrow's tender touch,
It dances with joy, igniting flames that clutch.
With vibrant melodies, it lifts our spirits high,
Invoking laughter and jubilance, reaching for the sky.

In its harmonious embrace, our existence finds meaning,
A sanctuary for the heart, where emotions find their leaning.
For music is the language that transcends all boundaries,
It speaks to the core of our souls, binding us in unity.

So let us immerse ourselves in this symphony divine,
Let its vibrant notes cleanse our spirits, intertwining mind and spine.
May we find solace in its rhythm, its healing energy so pure,
For in the language of music, our souls forever endure.

Section Two

In our daily lives, we often find ourselves caught up in the routines and expectations set before us. But let's take a moment to escape the ordinary and delve into the realm of boundless imagination. Together, let's craft poetry and weave tales that transport us to enchanting worlds untethered by stress and worries. In this realm, our minds, hearts, and souls are free to explore the depths of creativity, where endless possibilities await. So come dear friend, let us embark on this whimsical journey and unlock the wonders of our own imagination.

This poem tells the story of a meteor that travels through the vastness of space, carrying with it the ability to share tales and secrets of the universe. The meteor is described as a graceful traveler, leaving trails of stardust in its wake.

As it journeys through the cosmos, the meteor becomes a storyteller, whispering to planets, moons, and distant suns. It shares stories of love, loss, cosmic romances, and divine wisdom. It witnesses the birth of stars and the wonders of the universe, painting a vivid picture of the cosmos.

When the meteor reaches Earth, it becomes a source of inspiration and hope, gifting us with dreams and illuminating our souls. It reminds us of the infinite stories that exist within us and the universe, encouraging us to embrace our own narratives and explore the unknown.

Overall, the poem celebrates the power of storytelling and the beauty of the universe, inviting us to reflect on the stories we carry within ourselves and the interconnectedness of all things.

"Cosmic Chronicles: A Meteor's Odyssey"

In a realm of stars, where galaxies collide,
A tale of destiny, forever to abide.
A meteor streaked across the cosmic expanse,
Leaving trails of stardust in its graceful dance.

A traveler from afar, a celestial light,
Carrying secrets of the universe in its flight.
It soared through the darkness, a cosmic nomad,
Guided by constellations, its journey never sad.

Through boundless space, it traversed with grace,
A storyteller from the cosmos, leaving a trace.
Whispering to planets, sharing tales untold,

Unveiling mysteries, as the universe unfolds.

On distant worlds, it left its radiant mark,
Igniting hope in souls amid the shadows stark.
A witness to the birth of stars and galaxies anew,
This meteor, a storyteller, is forever true.

It whispered to the moon tales of love and loss,
Of cosmic romances and celestial gloss.
It spoke to distant suns, secrets of the divine,
Of ancient wisdom, etched in cosmic design.

Across nebulae and supernovae, it passed,
Unveiling the wonders of time, unsurpassed.
From black holes to pulsars, it painted the sky,
An interstellar narrative, soaring so high.

And as it reached our Earth, a beacon of Light,
It gifted us dreams in the stillness of night.
A cosmic storyteller, illuminating our souls,
Reminding us of the universe's infinite roles.

So, let us embrace this meteoric tale,
Let its story ignite our spirits, never frail.
For within its celestial journey, we find our own,
A reminder of the stories in our hearts, unknown.

In a world where imagination and wonder intertwine, let us embark on a journey through the eyes of a butterfly. From its humble beginnings as a caterpillar yearning for transformation to its emergence as a creature of ethereal grace, this tale takes us on a whimsical adventure. Through vibrant meadows and petals, the butterfly explores untrodden realms, witnessing tales of love, loss, and dreams. As the seasons change, it leaves behind a legacy, inspiring dreamers and igniting hope. So, join us as we delve into this tale, where imagination takes flight, and the butterfly's perspective fills our hearts with awe and wonder.

"Wings of Whimsy: A Butterfly's Tale"

In realms of dreams, where imagination takes flight,
Let me share my tale through the butterfly's insight.
From the very moment, I emerged, a caterpillar small,
I felt a stirring deep within, a whispering call.

Through lush emerald leaves, I feasted with delight,
Imagining the wonders that awaited in my flight.
I yearned for transformation, to be reborn anew,
To soar among the heavens in a world of vibrant hue.

Encased within my chrysalis, a realm of secret dreams,
Where I swam in colors, in kaleidoscopic streams.
A symphony of magic, a metamorphic embrace,
As I shed my earthly bindings, to embrace ethereal grace.

And as I emerged, a creature of wonder and awe,
My wings unfurled, a masterpiece I never foresaw.
A canvas painted by dreams, with strokes of fairy dust,
I marveled at my beauty in a world so robust.

I danced upon the zephyrs with grace and sheer delight,
Sampling nature's nectar from dawn until twilight.
Through meadows and valleys, I drifted on a breeze,
Exploring realms untrodden, where imagination sees.

In each petal's embrace, a secret world unveiled,
Where tiny creatures whispered, and floral stories trailed.
Oh, the tales I've witnessed, as I soared through the sky,
Of love and loss, of dreams that fluttered by.

But as the seasons changed, I felt time's gentle pull,
A melancholic whisper, a farewell to the colorful.
Yet, fear not for my essence, dear friends, it carries on,
In the hearts of dreamers, as inspiration spawns.

For I am more than just a butterfly, ephemeral and bright,
I am a symbol of hope, a beacon in the night.
So let your imagination soar, let wonder be your guide,

Embrace the magic within, let your spirit take pride.

In the story of my life, let your own dreams unfurl,
For the butterfly's tale is one of wonder and pearls.
And as I bid you adieu, in this whimsical rhyme,
May your life be a butterfly's, a dance through space and time.

This poem invites you to embark on a journey of contemplation and reflection. It explores the realm of philosophers, those enigmatic thinkers who seek answers to profound questions. The poem ponders what makes a philosopher and delves into the depths of their minds, their insatiable curiosity, and their hunger to question and unfold the mysteries of existence.

It highlights the philosophers' role as alchemists of thought, distilling and refining ideas that transcend time. Their profound thoughts, like stars, illuminate the night, guiding seekers of truth toward enlightenment. The poem also raises the question of where these profound thoughts take birth, whether in moments of solitude or amidst worldly experiences.

Ultimately, the poem invites you to marvel at the philosophers' quest as they unravel the tapestry of human life. It emphasizes the wisdom and guidance that philosophers offer as we seek understanding and strive to find our place in the world. In the realm of philosophers, we find solace and strength as they unravel the secrets of day and night, leading us to a world of enlightenment where truths are spread.

"Wisdom's Horizon: A Philosophical Odyssey"

In the vast expanse of intellectual seas,
Where profound thoughts dance upon the breeze,
Resides the realm of philosophers, profound and wise,
Seeking answers to questions that make us realize.

What makes a philosopher, this enigmatic breed,
With minds that ponder, like a soaring steed?
Is it the spark of curiosity, a flame in their soul,
Or the insatiable hunger to question and unfold?

From the depths of ancient wisdom, they arise,
Challenging the norms that bind our minds,
With metaphors and allegories, they dare to explore,
The mysteries of existence, at its very core.
Like alchemists of thought, they distill and refine,

Ideas that transcend the limits of time,
From Plato's cave to Nietzsche's abyss,
They grapple with concepts, forging mental bliss.

Their thoughts, like stars, illuminate the night,
Guiding seekers of truth towards the Light,
Through rigorous debate and dialectical strife,
They unravel the tapestry of human life.

Yet, where do these profound thoughts take birth,
In the recesses of solitude or amidst worldly mirth?
Do they emerge from poignant moments of despair,
Or in moments of ecstasy, suspended in the air?

Perhaps it's in the realms of introspection profound,
Where the philosopher's mind begins to astound,
In the depths of solitude, they find their muse,
Weaving poetic notions, they cannot refuse.

So let us marvel at the philosophers' quest,
As they ponder the mysteries, ever obsessed,
For it is their wisdom that guides us along,
As we seek understanding, to where we belong.

In the realm of philosophers, we find solace and might,
As they unravel the secrets of day and night,
Through their deep and intense thoughts, we are led,
To a world of enlightenment, where truths are spread.

In the depths of a forgotten forest, where sunlight barely pierces through the dense canopy, lies a hidden clearing. It is a place untouched by time, where magic lingers in the air and whispers of ancient secrets are carried on the wind. Tall, towering trees surround the clearing, their branches intertwining like guardians protecting the mystical realm within. The ground is carpeted with a vibrant tapestry of moss, soft and inviting to the touch. Rays of golden light filter through the gaps in the foliage, creating an ethereal glow that dances upon the forest floor. It is in this enchanted sanctuary that our journey begins, where imagination knows no bounds, and the extraordinary awaits.

"Elysium of Imagination: A World Crafted in Dreams"

In a world of endless possibilities,
Where imagination reigns with ease,
My fantasies come alive, untamed and free,
A realm created solely by me.

A land of vibrant colors and surreal sights,
Where gravity bends, and reality takes flight,
Creatures of my own design roam the land,
With features unique, and forms so grand.

In this realm, time is merely a suggestion,
Where moments stretch into eternal progression,
I dance with stars on a moonlit stage,
And converse with ancient sages.

I wander through enchanted forests deep,
Where trees whisper secrets they keep,
The leaves rustle with a magical symphony,
As I explore the wonders hidden within each tree.

Mountains rise with majestic grace,
Their peaks kissed by clouds, a heavenly embrace,
I climb their heights, conquering fear,
With each step, drawing closer to the atmosphere.

Beneath the surface, an ocean vast,
Where mermaids swim, their beauty unsurpassed,
I dive into depths surrounded by coral reefs,
In the company of creatures beyond belief.

In this fantasy world, I have the power,
To shape reality, like a masterful artist's hour,
I conjure dreams with a thought or a word,
And watch them unfold like a song to be heard.

But even in this realm of my own creation,
I yearn for connection, a shared sensation,
For the beauty of fantasies is when they are shared,

With kindred souls who understand and care.

So let us journey together, hand in hand,
Through the wonders of this imaginary land,
Where dreams become our reality, bold and bright,
Creating a world where all is made right.

Here in this next passage, describes an experience in the world of dreams. Where transported to a place of pure joy and innocence, where the feeling of weightlessness and joining in the merriment, running, jumping, and dancing with abandon. The dreamscape is filled with vibrant colors, laughter, and singing, evoking childhood memories of carefree play. In this realm, there are no worries or constraints, only endless possibilities and unadulterated fun. The scenes of their childhood dreams unfold, taking place in familiar locations like a park, with swings, games of tag, and the scent of ice cream in the air. The dreamscape also includes a treasure hunt through secret gardens and encounters with fairies. The dreams reach a climax in a grand ballroom, where the speaker dances and laughs with others, completely immersed in the joy of the moment. This dreamscape represents a place where time doesn't matter, where imaginations run wild, and where the innocence of childhood is treasured. The speaker carries the warmth and happiness of these dreams with them as they fall into a peaceful slumber.

In the world of dreams, I find myself transported to a place of pure joy and innocence. Colors swirl around me, vibrant and alive, as laughter and singing fill the air. I feel weightless as if my feet are barely touching the ground, and I join in the merriment, running, jumping, and dancing with abandon. The melodies of childhood reverberate through my being, awakening long-forgotten memories of carefree days spent in play. In this dream realm, there are no worries or constraints, only endless possibilities and pure, unadulterated fun. The echoes of laughter and the rhythm of our footsteps mix harmoniously, creating a symphony of happiness that resonates within me. It is a place where time stands still, where the worries of the world fade away, and all that matters is the sheer delight of being alive.

As I continue to drift deeper into slumber, the scenes of my childhood dreams unfold before me like a vivid tapestry. I find myself in familiar places, the ones I used to frequent as a child. The park, with its towering trees and sprawling green fields, becomes the backdrop for our adventures. The swings creak and sway, beckoning us to soar higher and higher into the cerulean sky. The sound of children's laughter fills the air, contagious and pure, as we chase each other in a game of tag.

The sun shines brightly, casting a warm glow that illuminates the joyous expressions on our faces. The air is tinged with the scent of freshly cut grass and the sweet aroma of ice cream wafting from the nearby vendor. We gather in a circle, holding hands, as we engage in a lively game of Duck

Goose. The excitement builds as we take turns, giggling with anticipation, until finally, someone is chosen as the "goose" and races around the circle, trying to catch the next unsuspecting victim.

Our energy seems boundless as we embark on a treasure hunt, following the whimsical clues that lead us through hidden nooks and crannies of our imaginary world. We stumble upon secret gardens teeming with vibrant flowers and mystic creatures. Fairies flutter around us, leaving trails of glitter in their wake, their delicate wings glimmering in the sunlight. We skip along a babbling brook, imagining it to be a river in a faraway land.

As we reach the climax of our dreamscape, we find ourselves in a grand ballroom adorned with twinkling lights and colorful streamers. Music fills the air, and we twirl and spin in time with the rhythm, our feet barely touching the polished floor. Laughter echoes throughout the room, merging with the melody, creating a symphony of pure bliss. The world outside fades away, and all that exists in this moment is the sheer joy of being in each other's company.

In this enchanting realm of dreams, time is irrelevant. We lose ourselves in the delight of the present, cherishing every moment, every shared laugh, and every dance step. We are free to be our authentic selves, unrestricted by the boundaries of reality. It is a place where our imaginations run wild, where dreams come to life, and where the innocence of childhood is preserved. And as I finally drift into a peaceful slumber, I carry with me the warmth and happiness of these childhood dreams, knowing that they will always be a cherished part of who I am.

My dear reader, step into the realm of the Matrix Fantasy, where the boundaries of imagination are shattered, and dreams take flight. Here, you are invited to unleash your creative spirit and embark on a journey through a tapestry of wonders. Let your mind wander through enchanted landscapes, encounter mythical creatures, and delve into the depths of your wildest dreams. Embrace the power of this digital realm, where you have the freedom to shape your own narrative and explore the limitless possibilities that await. So, come forth and immerse yourself in this fantastical realm, where the only limit is the depth of your imagination. Embellish this Matrix fantasy and let your imagination soar to new heights.

"Whispers of the Digital Realm: A Matrix Odyssey"

In a realm beyond our own, a world of dreams untold,
Where reality blurs and wonders unfold.
There lies a place, both mystical and grand,
A tapestry woven by a masterful hand.

Welcome, dear traveler, to the Matrix divine,
Where fantasy dances and fantasies entwine.
A realm where dreams take flight, unbound by time,
A symphony of illusions, a place so sublime.

In this ethereal realm, where possibilities bloom,
Imagination reigns, and visions consume.
Colors swirl and shimmer, vibrant and bright,
As reality bends and takes flight in the night.

Here, the laws of reason are gently set aside,
And the mind's eye is free to explore far and wide.
A kaleidoscope of wonders unfolds before your gaze,
As whispers of enchantment trail through the haze.

Within this digital tapestry, secrets are revealed,
Hidden realms and treasures waiting to be unsealed.
Mystical creatures roam in lands unknown,
Unfolding stories with every step they've sown.

The Matrix whispers tales of heroes brave,
Of knights in shining armor, who rise to save.
They face dragons fierce and demons dark,
Their courage igniting a triumphant spark.

In this fantastical realm, where dreams intertwine,
You'll find castles of emerald and rivers divine.
You'll sail through skies on the wings of a dove,
And dance on moonbeams with the ones you love.

But beware, dear traveler, of the illusions that sway,
For the Matrix can be both night and day.
As shadows creep and darkness seeps,

Remember, in dreams, the mind is what it keeps.

So, wander, dear traveler with an open heart,
Embrace the wonders that this Matrix imparts.
Let your imagination soar like a bird in flight,
And lose yourself in the magic, both day and night.

For the Matrix is a portal, a gateway to dreams,
Where reality is but a thread, or so it seems.
So, venture forth, dear traveler, with wonder and glee,
And let the Matrix's charm set your spirit free.

Section Three

"Thoughts in Technicolor"

In the realm where thoughts collide,
A kaleidoscope of colors reside.
Emotions dance in vibrant hues,
A symphony of thoughts, diverse and true.

In technicolor, they come alive,
A tapestry of feelings, ready to thrive.
Reds of passion, burning with desire,
Blues of calmness, like a soothing choir.

Golden yellows, a burst of joy,
Greens of envy, a feeling to deploy.
Purples of mystery, tinged with intrigue,
Oranges of warmth, like a comforting league.

Thoughts in technicolor, they intertwine,
A fusion of emotions, both yours and mine.
A palette of perspectives, a vivid array,
Where contradictions coexist and play.

In each stroke of color, a story unfolds,
A glimpse into minds, untold and bold.
Perspicacity gleams, wisdom takes flight,
As thoughts in technicolor ignite the night.

With every verse, a new layer unfurls,
A canvas painted with the thoughts of the world.
From the depths of sorrow to the heights of glee,
Thoughts in technicolor set our minds free.

So let us celebrate this vibrant blend,
Where emotions and thoughts transcend.
In this poem's embrace, let us unite,
Thoughts in technicolor, a kaleidoscope of Light.

"Whispers of the Soul"

In the depths of my mind, a symphony unfurls,
Whispers of the soul, where dreams and fears twirl.
A reflection of my being, a tapestry of thought,
Where aspirations and worries are intricately wrought.

Within this symphony, diverse and vast,
Lies a symphony of fears, haunting and steadfast.
They whisper softly, like shadows in the night,
Seeking to dim the spark that yearns for Light.

One whisper speaks of doubt, a crippling fear,
That my dreams are futile, never meant to be near.
But I silence this whisper, with courage in my heart,
For dreams are meant to be pursued, a vital part.

Another whisper echoes, a fear of the unknown,
Of stepping into the abyss, where certainty is blown.
But I embrace this fear, a catalyst for growth,
For it is through challenges we discover our oath.

Yet amidst these fears, aspirations arise,
Whispers that uplift like wings ready to rise.
A whisper of passion, burning deep within,
Guiding me towards the path where I can begin.

A whisper of purpose, a calling from the soul,
To make a difference, to play a vital role.
In this vast symphony, I find my truest voice,
A melody of aspirations, a song of rejoice.

The whisper of love, tender and pure,
To connect with others, to make hearts endure.
To spread compassion, like a gentle breeze,
Bringing warmth and solace, putting minds at ease.

Oh, the whispers of the soul, how they intertwine,
A dance of dreams and fears, a rhythm so fine.
They paint the canvas of our innermost core,

Shaping who we are and what we stand for.

So, let the symphony play, with all its might,
Embrace the whispers, both dark and light.
For within this reflection, our true selves reside,
A tapestry of dreams and fears, forever intertwined.

"Reflections of the Unseen"

In the depths of the unseen, where shadows play,
Lies a story untold, hidden away.
You think you know me, but you cannot see,
The pain and struggles that reside within me.

Reflections of the unseen, they dance and sway,
Revealing fragments of a life astray.
Each unspoken truth, a weight on my soul,
A burden I carry that takes its toll.

Behind the smile, a river of tears,
Washing away the hopes and the fears.
In the quiet moments, when no one is near,
I confront the demons that I hold dear.

The scars on my heart, they tell a tale,
Of battles fought and dreams that fell.
But you, with your assumptions, cannot perceive,
The depths of my sorrow, the pain I conceive.
In the corners of my mind, secrets reside,
Whispers of anguish I often hide.
The world sees a facade, a mask so bright,
But underneath, a darkness fights.

Reflections of the unseen, they beg to be heard,
To unravel the mysteries like a wounded bird.
But the words remain trapped, imprisoned within,
Aching for release, for the truth to begin.

So, do not judge me with your narrow view,
For the unseen, my struggles are known to few.

In the silence of my mind, I find solace and peace,
A sanctuary where my secrets find release.

This mean poem reflects the pain I bear,
The unseen battles that brought me here.
So, before you judge, pause and reflect,
For the unseen depths, you cannot detect.

"Puzzle of Perspectives"

In the depths of my being, a fire burns bright,
Igniting my spirit with passion and insight.
I navigate this journey, a vessel of emotions,
Seeking connection, fostering heartfelt devotions.

Through the tapestry of life, I weave my own thread,
Intertwined with others, our stories widespread.
I listen with intent to the whispers of souls,
Their joys and sorrows, their triumphs and tolls.

In the heartache of loss, I've shed tears like rain,
Bearing witness to grief, shared in collective pain.
Yet through shared vulnerability, we find solace,
An unspoken bond in the depths of our promise.

With every encounter, a chance to grow,
To bridge divides and let compassion flow.
For we are but fragments in a vast cosmic scheme,
Yet together, we create a tapestry of dreams.

So let us embrace our humanness, our flaws and grace,
Embrace the raw beauty in each unique face.
For it is in our shared stories, our heartfelt connection,
That we find the true essence of love and reflection.

"Journeys of Imagination: Where Legends Unite"

Embark on fantastical journeys where dreams intertwine,
Old heroes, warriors, and gods of lore in realms so divine.
Within the depths of my being, imagination takes hold,
Unleashing tales of ancient valor, both daring and bold.

Through enchanted forests, where King Arthur's knights reside,
I join their noble quest, with honor as my guide.
Excalibur gleams in my hand, a weapon forged in myth,
Together we battle darkness, restoring hope's sweet pith.

In the company of Hercules, I learn strength untold,
Facing monstrous challenges, both mighty and bold.
With lion's mane and club in hand, we conquer every plight,
Defying the odds, as heroes do, in the realm of might.

Amidst the stars, I soar beside Thor, the God of thunder,
His mighty hammer, Mjolnir, breaking worlds asunder.
We traverse cosmic realms, protecting realms afar,
Battling cosmic adversaries, guided by a shining star.

Alongside Athena, goddess of wisdom and war,
I delve into the depths of knowledge, seeking truth's core.
Her owl perched upon my shoulder, a guide so wise and bright,
Together we unravel mysteries in the realm of intellectual Light.

These figures of legend, cast in tales of old,
Guide me on journeys where heroes' spirits unfold.
Their stories intertwine with my own desires and dreams,
Creating a tapestry where reality and myth gleam.

In these imaginative adventures, authenticity is found,
As the essence of heroes and gods forever resound.
So let us embark on these mystical flights,
Where legends unite and imagination ignites.

"Inkblots of Identity"

In the realm of a page, inkblots dance and play,
A kaleidoscope of colors, where identities find their way.
Each droplet of ink, a fragment of who we are,
A tapestry of experiences, both near and far.

I am the warrior, fierce and bold,
Battle scars etched upon my soul; stories yet untold.
With sword in hand, I march to face life's strife,
Defending my truth, seeking purpose in this life.

I am the poet, my words a gentle breeze,
Whispering melodies of love, sorrow, and unease.
In rhymes and verses, I paint emotions untamed,
Inviting you to feel, to wander, to be unashamed.

I am the scientist, curious and keen,
Exploring mysteries unknown, realms yet unseen.
In the depths of discovery, my mind takes flight,
Unraveling the secrets of the universe, day and night.

I am the wanderer with feet that never tire,
Roaming landscapes vast, my spirit soaring higher.
In each new horizon, I find fragments of my soul,
Absorbing cultures, connecting, making myself whole.

I am the dreamer, lost in realms of fantasy,
Where imagination thrives, boundless and free.
In worlds of my creation, I mold reality anew,
Inviting you to wander, to dream, to pursue.

In the inkblots that stain this canvas of mine,
I celebrate the uniqueness, the colors that define,
The beauty of a tapestry, woven thread by thread,
Where individuality thrives, where souls are truly fed.
So come, dear reader, immerse yourself in this scene,
Let inkblots of identity paint your own dreams.
Embrace the kaleidoscope, the vastness of your own being,
For in this realm of words, we are forever freeing.

"Whispers of the Kaleidoscope"

In distant lands, a friendship blooms,
A tale of fate, where destiny looms.
Through time and space, they're bound,
A bond unbreakable, profound.

Exploring thoughts desires anew,
A journey within they pursue.
Through poetry's lens, they confide,
The kaleidoscope of thoughts inside.

A symphony of colors, vibrant and bright,
Unveiling worlds, both day and night.
With each word penned, a story unfolds,
Whispers of the kaleidoscope, it beholds.

In whispers, secrets are shared,
A kaleidoscope of dreams bared.
Through poetry's embrace, they find,
The kaleidoscope within, unconfined.

Each verse a brushstroke, painting a scene,
Of love, loss, and places unseen.
The power of words, a catalyst profound,
Transforming hearts without a sound.

Friendship's tapestry, woven with care,
Threads of connection, beyond compare.
Through the kaleidoscope's lens, they see,
The beauty of unity, hearts set free.

And as the journey draws to an end,
Their voices blend, harmonious blend.
For in this tapestry, a truth remains,
The kaleidoscope's magic forever sustains.

So let us honor this merging of souls,
A testament to how poetry consoles.
Through friendship's embrace, we rise,

"The Kaleidoscope Mind: Embracing the Diversities in Poetic Collective" By Deanna F Starr

A kaleidoscope of dreams reaching the skies.

Expanding horizons, they dare to explore,
Through poetic landscapes, forevermore.
In verses woven, they find solace and peace,
As their kaleidoscope of thoughts increase.

They delve deeper into the realms of the mind,
Seeking treasures of wisdom, rare to find.
With ink-stained hands, they write their tales,
Unveiling the kaleidoscope that never pales.

Through laughter and tears, they stand as one,
Their friendship like the moon and sun.
In this vast universe, they find their place,
A kaleidoscope of love, space, and grace.

They traverse the valleys of sorrow and pain,
Writing verses that heal, like gentle rain.
Their words hold power, like a sacred chant,
In the kaleidoscope's embrace, they enchant.

With every line, a new world unfolds,
A symphony of emotions, untold.
The kaleidoscope's dance, a vibrant display,
In the realm of poetry, they forever sway.

And when the final verse is penned,
Their journey, though complete, will never end.
For the kaleidoscope's magic, eternally true,
In their hearts, their friendship will renew.

So let us celebrate this bond they share,
A tapestry woven with love and care.
Through the whispers of the kaleidoscope's rhyme,
Their friendship endures, transcending time.

The themes of friendship, self-exploration, the power of poetry, and the kaleidoscope metaphor are expanded upon. The poem celebrates the journey of us all as we dive deeper into our thoughts and emotions, discovering new worlds and finding solace in our words.

The kaleidoscope symbolizes the vastness and beauty of our shared experiences, and the poem emphasizes the eternal nature of our friendships.

Let's marvel for a moment at the fascinating likeness between a kaleidoscope and a prism. They both rely on Light to weave enchanting displays of color and intricate patterns, just as our own lives are shaped by the moments that illuminate and color them. It's a captivating analogy that draws us in, highlighting the profound and transformative influence of our experiences and the incredible beauty that arises from them.

"Celestial Reverie: Wonders of the Universe"

Beneath the jeweled blanket of the night,
Where stars ignite the boundless sky,
Whispers of cosmic tales take flight,
In galaxies, where dreams abide.

Each constellation, a celestial muse,
Weaving stories with celestial grace,
In silent symphonies, they gently infuse,
The wonder of the universe, embracing space.

A moonbeam dance in the midnight air,
Unveiling secrets, ancient, rare,
Echoes of time, in shimmering Light,
A cosmic ballet enchanting the night.

Behold the world with eyes aglow,
Radiant wonders, in nature's glow,
Mountains rise, and oceans wade,
As the Earth spins its serenade.

Each petal's bloom, a masterpiece in part,
A tapestry woven with nature's art,
For in every breath, a world unfolds,
Where the mystic and the mundane behold.

In each glance, a universe's gaze,
A portrait of wonder in an endless maze,
Immortal realms and ephemeral tides,

A story of awe that forever abides.

May this poem fill your heart with a sense of awe and wonder, and transport you to the realms of the extraordinary.

Kaleidoscope of Human Experience," a poetic odyssey that invites you to peer through the enchanting imagery of prisms and kaleidoscopes, igniting your imagination to envision the captivating vistas that unfold within each verse. Prepare to be immersed in a world where the myriad facets of human experience come alive, just as light dances through crystal, casting vibrant hues and infinite patterns upon the canvas of our lives. Embark on a journey through joy and sorrow, triumph and tribulation, where every twist and turn reflects the resplendent tapestry of our shared human existence. As you delve into these verses, embrace the intricate beauty of our collective stories and rejoice in the kaleidoscope of courage, love, and resilience that defines us. Let the imagery within these lines paint a picture that shimmers with the boundless colors of our shared human experience and inspires you to celebrate the awe-inspiring complexity of life.

"Prisms of Life: The Kaleidoscope of Human Experience."

Through prisms and kaleidoscopes, we see,
The myriad facets of life's symphony.
Like Light through crystal, our stories unfold,
In hues and patterns, both new and old.

Each twist and turn, a dance of fate,
Refracting moments, both small and great.
In every shard and every glimmer,
We find reflections, each one a shimmer.

A kaleidoscope of joys and fears,
Spinning through laughter, spinning through tears,
Every fragment, a tale to behold,
In boundless patterns, our lives unfold.

Like colors shifting in endless bloom,
Our ever-changing, transient plume,
Through trials and triumphs, we find our way,
In this grand kaleidoscope of every day.

Each prism of hope, a radiant gleam,
Illuminates the path of every dream.

"The Kaleidoscope Mind: Embracing the Diversities in Poetic Collective"   By Deanna F Starr

In sorrow's prism, a comforting light,
Guiding us through the darkest night.

As time refracts, we embrace the unknown,
Our lives, a spectrum of tales full-blown.
In love, in loss, through every embrace,
We find our reflections in life's intricate grace.

So let us cherish this wondrous sphere,
In all its facets, crystal clear.
For in our stories, both bright and infused,
We see humanity so beautifully diffused.

In every twist, in every view,
We find connection, both deep and true.
Our kaleidoscope of courage and strife,
Glimmers with the colors of our shared life.

I hope this poem captures the essence of the magnificent and varied experiences that make up the human journey, inspired by the imagery of prisms and kaleidoscopes.

In the poem "The Splendor of the Rainbow," we are invited to marvel at the captivating beauty of a rainbow. Through vivid descriptions of its vibrant hues, the poem explores the deeper meanings and emotions evoked by this natural wonder. It encourages us to embrace the various symbols and messages hidden within each color, reminding us to appreciate life's wonders and hold them close to our hearts. Prepare to be enchanted as we delve into the magical world of the rainbow.

"The Splendor of the Rainbow"

Have you ever stood in awe, my friend,
gazing at a rainbow's glorious blend?
In its vibrant hues, a story untold,
a tapestry of wonder, a sight to behold.

As sunlight dances with falling rain,
a kaleidoscope of colors, a heavenly stain.
Each droplet a prism, bending the Light,
revealing a spectacle, a mesmerizing sight.

First, a crimson arch, fiery and bold,
whispering tales of passion untold.
A symbol of courage, of love's fierce embrace,
inviting you to explore its hidden grace.

Next, an orange ribbon, vibrant and bright,
reflecting the warmth of a golden twilight.
A reminder of joy, zest and delight,
unleashing the child within, taking flight.

Then, a yellow curve, like sunshine's embrace,
radiating hope and optimism, a gentle pace.
With every step forward, a new beginning,
a chance to embrace life, its infinite glistening.

Followed by a verdant arc, lush and serene,
the color of growth, renewal and dream.
It beckons you to find solace in nature's embrace,
to seek harmony and find your rightful place.

Next, a sapphire arch, deep and serene,
whispering tales of wisdom, of visions unseen.
The color of truth, of knowledge untold,
It invites you to explore mysteries behold.

Then comes the indigo curve, mysterious and rare,
a bridge to the cosmos, a celestial affair.

With its cosmic depths, it sparks curiosity,
inviting you to delve into cosmic unity.

Lastly, a violet arc, serene and divine,
embodying grace, spiritual and kind.
It whispers of magic, of dreams coming true,
a reminder that miracles can happen to you.

Oh, dear friend, let the rainbow's allure,
invite your heart, your spirit, to endure.
In its intricate details, a world unfurled,
a reminder of life's wonders, a gift to behold.

So, next time you see a rainbow's embrace,
let it stir your soul; let it leave a trace.
For in its splendor, a message is clear,
to cherish life's colors, to hold them near.

Conclusion: A Tapestry of Gratitude

Dear reader,

As we draw the curtains on "The Kaleidoscope Mind: Embracing the Diversities in Poetic Collective," I extend my heartfelt gratitude for joining me on this thought-provoking journey. Through the varied hues and melodies of each poem, you've traversed realms of metamorphosis, resilience, and self-discovery.

In "Blossoming Souls: The Lotus Journey," you witnessed the unfolding of inner beauty, much like a lotus rising from the mud. "Unveiling Brilliance: The Gemstone Journey" offered insights into the precious facets that make each soul unique, while "The Resilient Light" illuminated the transformative power within.

The tapestry of mistakes in "The Tapestry of Mistakes" became stepping stones to greatness, echoing the triumph of self-acceptance. In "The Dance of Friendships," you waltzed through connections that shaped growth, while "Unveiling the Divine" beckoned a journey of self-discovery.

The caregiver's odyssey in "Garden of Compassion" and the metamorphosis in the revised poem "Harmony Unveiled" portrayed the harmony found in caregiving. "Love's Tapestry" wove an enchanting prelude, and "Dance of Life" painted a tapestry balancing work, love, and dreams.

As cosmic chronicles unfolded in "A Meteor's Odyssey" and "Elysium of Imagination" crafted worlds in dreams, you voyaged through realms of whimsy and philosophical musings. "Whispers of the Digital Realm" invites you into a matrix odyssey, exploring the wonders of the digital tapestry.

In the kaleidoscope of thought-provoking poems in Section Three, from "Thoughts in Technicolor" to "The Splendor of the Rainbow," you glimpsed into the prisms of life, the whispers of the soul, and the celestial reverie of the universe.

Now, as you step away from these verses, I thank you for allowing these words to resonate within. May the tapestry of my collective thoughts linger in your mind, inspiring great reflections and invoking moments of wonder.

With sincere gratitude and wishes for a tapestry of great thoughts,
Deanna F Starr

Printed in Great Britain
by Amazon